How To Start A Drop Shipping Business

Make Your First $1,000
Using This Powerful Drop
Shipping Business Model

By

Maxwell Rotheray

Table of Contents

CHAPTER ONE

Introduction

Drop shipping is an e-commerce supply chain management system in which a retailer operates without maintaining an inventory, but instead upon receipt of an order from customers, searches and forwards customers information to the right supplier, who delivers the goods to the customers.

Merchants who lack capital but desire to go into business take advantage of the benefits it offers:

I.   It is simple to set up
      What you have to do is to partner with a supplier, own a website and promote your drop shipping business

II.   The total estimated cost of starting a drop shipping business is reasonably low. The only cost associated with drop shipping is the cost of running your website (driving traffic to your website, hosting, website applications) where you have all the information about your drop shipping business.

III. Drop shipping risks are relatively low. You don't incur overhead costs such as renting a warehouse, no office, no employee, and so you can run your drop shipping business from anywhere.

IV. You are going to have a drop ship supplier for every business or product. Some people tend to worry much about finding a supplier, but drop shipping is the trend of the day, so every selling product must have a supplier. Customers will get their products without any hitch or delay. So, it makes life easy for any merchant who desires to go into drop shipping business.

V. You decide the scale of your dropship business. Traditionally, retailers who want to grow their businesses, put extra effort, invest more resources, but in dropship business, all you have to do is to drive more traffic to your website, and when the orders arrive, you alert the drop ship supplier who will deliver to the customer. Your profit will be earned disproportionately to your efforts.

VI.   Lower losses on goods that do not meet specifications

A retailer who delivers directly to the customer risks making some losses when goods damage on transit or fail to meet specifications because of longer shipment steps involved. But when goods are delivered directly from the dropship supplier, the likelihood of goods damaging on transit is reduced. However, there are inherent weaknesses associated with drop shipping business

These demerits cover things like lower profit margin, a greater liability when there is a serious problem. This problem can be a failure to supply, or goods are damaged in transit, or the goods fall short of a specification. In this case, since the contract of sale of goods is between the retailer and the customer, the retailer bears the full brunt of the liability. The retailer takes a smaller profit margin because the supplier charges a higher price for drop shipping goods. The level of competition of drop shipping products can be very high while certain issues are likely to arise due to the complex nature of drop shipping. Amongst the challenges may include competition amongst product suppliers. There might be more than one supplier of the same product. In this circumstance, the retailer may work out and pay the shipping costs separately, and if these shipping costs are transferred to the customer, may have a negative effect on the conversion rates, as well impacting on the profit margin of your drop shipping business.

"If you are not willing to risk the usual, you will have to settle for the ordinary."

-Jim Rohn

CHAPTER TWO

How Drop Shipping Works

The drop shipping business is a simple process, involving a tripartite business. The first is a retailer, who buys from the manufacturer/wholesaler.

The second is the supplier/ wholesaler who supplies directly to the customer

The third is the customer who orders the products that are supplied.

To set up a drop shipping business, the first thing is to select the products you are interested in, as a retailer and partner with manufacturers/wholesalers that stock such products. You will have to set up a website which will showcase your products and use all manners of marketing gimmicks to drive traffic to your site. As a retailer, you will have to market your products all over the USA and beyond. The order will likely come through your website.

Your partner, be it a manufacturer or wholesaler will be ready to ship the product to the customer direct.

On the active part, an order is being received from a customer. The order information will be received by the retailer and passed to the wholesaler or manufacturer. From there, the products will be arranged and shipped to the customer according to the information provided by the retailer.

The three-stage process is as follows: the customer, who browses the web and finds out that a particular drop ship retailer has the products the customer is interested in. The customer then sends information to the retailer, who signs a trade contract with the customer, and the customer's details are passed on to the manufacturer/wholesaler.

The wholesaler upon the receipt of the order arranges for the order to be supplied on behalf of the retailer.

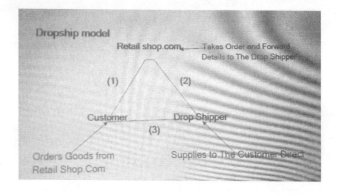

14

"All progress takes place outside the comfort zone." -Michael John Bobak

CHAPTER THREE

How Much You Can Make

Drop shipping, like most businesses, takes a lot of hard work to make headway and start making a profit. Those who understand online marketing can research on the target market, competitors and the products that are likely to be beneficial to the customer, it takes them few weeks, if not months to start making their sales. For instance, before you launch your drop shipping retail store, you would have done the following:

I. Extensive research on your target market, products you want to trade on, suppliers/wholesalers you want to partner with, competitors and the likely demand.

II. Have a perfect website in terms of pictures, good descriptions, processing of shipping documents, fair return policies and guarantees.

III. Select your promotional tools for social media.

IV. Install the social Rabbit Plugin to manage your social media marketing automatically and connect to the stores' social media.

V. Connect additional plugins that will help manage the website.

VI. Always research on the product and add the ones that are likely to be profitable.

VII. Conclude on your pricing policies and strategies

VIII. Launch your promotional campaign

IX. Update your website where necessary

X. Review your pricing strategies as time goes on.

XI. Update your product offers and review their prices.

The above may seem very hard for a beginner, but as I said, if you want to make money from drop shipping in the first year of operation, you must be highly equipped.

It must be said that generally (8/10) of new businesses fail in the first few months, only about 3% last longer than 5 years. In drop shipping, however, only about (1/30) one out of thirty dropship business survive and grow exceedingly well after six months. In fact, 2-3/10 will break even (state of business where revenue and cost are equal, no profit nor loss). This is largely due to the misconception of and partly to the underestimating to what is involved in the drop shipping business.

So, if you dabble into the business without proper preparation (researching of likely demands, products, suppliers, competitors, and equally important, resources, you are more likely to fail.

So how much can you make?

On average, the profit margin for drop shipping business varies from 15% to 45%. However, that does not mean that all products have the same profit margin. Mainly consumer durables and luxury goods such as electronics, jewelry, have higher profit margins of up to 80% to 100%. It all boils down to finding the right product/niche and right supplier and going into a market that is not overly overfull. You can also try to grow your profit margin by sourcing for products directly from manufacturers instead of from wholesalers and other vendors.

"I failed myself to success."

-Thomas Edison

CHAPTER FOUR

How To Find A Profitable Niche/Product

It is really a daunting task finding profitable drop shipping products since every year about 250,000 new products make their way to the market place, but unfortunately, only about 5-15% survive. Even though the eCommerce giants such as Amazon, Alibaba and eBay make up to 34% or there-about of products sold from drop shipping, a starter or even an existing drop shipping company cannot attain such feat. So, we should look into areas where you can find profitable products for your drop shipping business. I will take you to step by step; whether you are a starter in online marketing or you are restructuring your existing online stores, looking for profitable products to add, there is a place for you in this write-up. Finding new products is a continuous exercise, what is important is that you must be unique in your choice, you must stay alert, and you keep on experimenting with new products. I list below the features or what I would call your guiding principles of what you should take into consideration when making your choice of products to sell.

a) Unique in some way

Unique products shouldn't be easily available in a brick and mortar shops around your area, and also there should not have a similar clone available

b) Not easily available

The product should be difficult to find. The point is that if the product is unique, people will surely go for it, making a demand for it to be high. So many online stores will look for it to introduce in their range of products in their stores, so you must take the lead and introduce it first and rake in the high ROI before others follow afterward.

c) Very difficult to find the price

Online stores that buy their products from AliExpress, the prices of such products cannot be traced by the consumers of online products. So, make every effort that customers cannot easily trace the prices of the products.

d) The products are not available within the country.

The products should not be sold within the country, and if the brick and mortar stores sell them, you are not likely to attract enough demand for them.

e) The high mark-up is available

The selling price that is common on drop shipping products ranges between $8 and $38. Simply put, people can easily spend this range of amount on online purchases, and when the prices go up higher, they are not likely to spend money above this range. The very known theory is that people shop on impulse, i.e. without planning in advance before the purchase is made, so they can spend any amount below $40

Before you make up your mind on the products to select, take advantage of the advice below:-

I.   Finding product ideas

The first step to take is to browse some of the profitable online stores to find out the products they are dealing on and what are their margins. You must sit with your team to screen out and evaluate the products you have come up with. The idea here is to discover the bestselling products, the trending products, and even the slow-moving lines to decide what you are going to include or exclude in your drop shipping business. If you are a starter, you can scale down the products to about 10

II.   Visit online community sites

Online community sites can be very useful because they do display relevant product behavior, interests, and opinions that are relevant to your needs. Facebook has such an online community site you visit.

III.   Social shopping sites

There are some social shopping sites out there you can visit to look at what the social community is recommending. Here you read the opinions of people with similar interests and see what product ideas you can get. Available social shopping sites include Pinterest and Fancy

IV.   Local Communities.

Visit your local communities trade shows, bazaars, thrift and co-operative societies, who knows, and you may find the products that be of interest to you.

V.   Hit and miss strategy

Find new products by going to AliExpress flash deals page and browse for products that are trending, make your selection of what you find there.

"If you can dream it, you can do it. If you can imagine it, you can have it."

-Walt Disney

CHAPTER FIVE

Realistic Drop Shipping Start-Up Budget

The journey to every business is not easy both in resource commitment and in personal efforts. The road to starting this business is never smooth, easy and even cheap no matter the products you have chosen to deal on. So, if you have made up your mind to go into drop shipping, there is a great need to spend some money even at the infancy stage of setting up the business. The question is, how much must you spend to go into the drop shipping online stores business?

The amount of money required to start the dropship business cannot be estimated with every amount of certainty. Some people have advocated $0 budget, others have said no, there must be some level of start-up cost that must be incurred before you can take off.

It is also believed you can start an online drop shipping store with $0. This is possible if you can use social media groups to drive traffic to your online store. However, without a doubt, doing everything by yourself will be extremely time intensive. For an instant, Tim Kock has a successful drop shipping store without spending a dime during the start-up period. His website is Tim Kock-Don't Get Fancy.

If you are investing $0 during you, start up, inform your friends, relations, and people in your Facebook and What Sapp groups about your products and their benefits. You can write blog articles centering on your products or develop blogs that target your niche. Then direct people from your blog to your products on your website.

Let us see the steps it will take you to launch your drop ship online store and how much you are likely to spend.

i.   Initial product/niche research

This initial research to gauge the niche market and the products that will suit the market; it doesn't have to cost you anything since you conduct the research yourself.

ii.   Get a website and a web host

To create a website, you need the following to build an interactive website:

- A domain name
- Web host provider
- CMS – WordPress content management system
- AliDropship plugin
- Your creative effort

You must choose a good name your customers will always locate on your online store. The second thing you must do is to choose a domain provider who will host your website. This is simply the server for your website. You can always search for many of them on your own, evaluate them and make a selection. The cost of this is about $48 per annum.

The next hurdle is to build your website, which you can do by going to WordPress .org and downloading its software to your server. This software doesn't cost you a dime, can download it free of charge.

This is the time to bring in AliDropship plugin; this is where your online store is created, and you can start your online dropship business. The AliDropship plugin will cost you $89 as of 2017, so find out the current price.

Finally, you can customize your website to your taste. You don't pay yourself for your effort, so you spend nothing for it.

The total cost sums up to $137 (89+48)

The cost of finding suppliers and products and other marketing efforts are $0. This is free because you can use your smartphone to carry out a search on the internet and achieve good results.

"Make time for everything you want in life. If you can make time for it, you deserve its attention—the manifestation of your success."

-Anonymous

CHAPTER SIX

Best Products for Profit

There are so many products for drop shipping online eCommerce business that should be good for your business. Some of these products are trending, some have a low price, some are popular, but let us review the products you can drop ship and be profitable. I am going to use such criteria as the following:

1) It must be profitable
2) It must be in high demand
3) It is convenient to ship the products in terms of weight and size
4) It must have a low price
5) There is potential for repeat purchase
6) The supplier must be reputable.
7) Products that are not fragile but solid
8) Products that are going to be available in the foreseeable future.
9) You are going to be a sole distributor or have access to exclusive pricing

1). It must be profitable. You should choose products that have a good margin so that there is always profit whenever you sell. There are so many products out there that have good margin particularly goods imported from AliExpress

2). The dropship product must in high demand. This in effect means that the demand for the products must be constant, in season and out of season, even though the margin for such products are low. You can measure the rate of demand for your potential drop ship products by looking out to see how many are searching for the product online using Google search engine. Fortunately, Google makes available its search volume via the keyword tools.

3). Find the products that are convenient to transport (load and off-load) without getting damaged in transit. The products also must not be too heavy so that the cost of transportation may be low.

4). The products must have low price   Low price, in this case, means that the products must be low priced so potential customers can buy them without a second thought, i.e., impulse buying.

5). There is potential for repeat purchase. The products should have the potential for repeat purchase; in other words, the products must be solid in terms of style, quality, craftsmanship, and durability. With these qualities, the products have the potential for attracting repeat purchase.

6). The supplier must be reputable. The supplier/manufacturer must be well known, locally and internationally.   The manufacturer/supplier reputation must not be in doubt and probably must have other products in its range of products.

7). Products must not be fragile. The product here must not be too fragile such as glassware or some electrical/electronic products.   The reason for this is that the incidence of product returns are going to be high, and this will eat into your profit.

8) The products must have the potential for being available in the market in the foreseeable future. Such products should be in the range of consumer durables such as mobile phone, camera, cooking utensils, etc.

9) You are the sole distributor or have access to exclusive prices. If you can negotiate your price, you are likely to make a substantial profit from your dropship business, though the problem is that other drop shippers may have similar access to similar products.

10) Go for a niche where you can add value If you cannot beat your competitors on price, solve your customers' problems in a particular way such as educating them with exceptional content. If your customers are happy with the solution you provide for

them through good content, that is what will attract them to your products.

11) Choose products with accessories. A product with accessories gives you more profit. The main product may not attract a good margin, but the accessory does. For example, a TV flat screen may be sold for $650, the HDMI cable that accompanies the TV may be sold for $35. Without mincing words, the $35 price commands about 500% mark-up. Though the problem really is how many TV you are going to sell and even if you sell the cable at $35 and make 500% mark-up, how much does it add to your profit.

With the total grasp of the above criteria for choosing the right product for your dropship eCommerce business, let me lead you into the products proper.

In addition to the above criteria listed above, you must do more research — Surf online market places such as eBay, Amazon, and AliExpress. Look out for product trends and how many players are active in selling the product in a particular niche. What is their profit margins, the shipping costs as well as the seller fees? With all these, you will be able to make a good choice of drop shipping products you want to deal on in 2019.

1). Crystal Water Bottles

First things first. This unique drop shipping product is very popular, and it comes with crystals attached to the base of the bottle, believe it or not, it has some spiritual effects. The Google trends graph puts it in the forefront since it indicates the number of people that are searching for the products

2). Microwave steam cleaner

This portable device is simple to operate. Just add water and vinegar into the cleaner, put it in the microwave for about 8 minutes and watch how the stains and crud from the microwaves disappear. After that, clean up the microwave, store away the cleaner until you need it again.

The simplicity of cleaning your microwave is what you should focus on in your marketing campaigns.

3) Laser hair removal

Some hairs in some part of your body is stubborn and cannot easily go until you match their stubbornness with Laser Hair Removal. This is a trending product, and people are talking widely about it. The good news is that the overall sales on it are accelerating and Google Trends even admit that searches for 'remove hair is going up. If you add this product to your range, you only need to market it; the buyer will come in their numbers because they will know what you sell a quality product.

4). Artificial Hair

Some women who are unable to grow their own hair use artificial hair to make it up. The truth is that they can fix artificial hair flawlessly into their own hairs. These products are in great demand and if you choose to add to your 2019 drop shipping product, you will earn a reasonable income from it.

5). Wireless phone chargers

The mystery of Wireless Phone Chargers still stuns many people. Some people just want to have the experience and want to try them out. In your 2019 product range, include it, compromise on quality, charge no less than necessary, customers will come in their numbers. Since such products are readily available, your customers can easily recommend their friends to you. Moreover, since the new iPhones are launched with wireless chargers, the demand for wireless chargers will continue to rise.

6). Phone Lenses

Fewer and fewer people are no longer using Smartphones and therefore it is a question of time, not smartphones will be phased out. If you love taking pictures, you might not be expected to buy an expensive camera when you are not a professional photographer, the alternative is to get a phone lens and fix it to your smartphone, and you are taking sharp photographs. The only thing you have to do is, when purchasing lenses, insist on those giving quality photographs. Customers will come in their numbers asking for more.

7). Car Phone Holder

The sales for car phone holder, has risen sharply since people driving must make use of their phone at any giving opportunity. You do not know when that important call will arrive and so you must be ready to take your call even if you are driving. But you must be careful when you are driving because of the inherent dangers in answering phones call while driving. This is where car phone holder fits in and it is also very useful when you want direction to where you are going. Having to start searching for your phone while driving poses a serious risk to the driver and other passengers. You can sell this item in your eCommerce drop shipping stores or in your car accessories store.

8). iPhone Repair Kit

iPhone cost a lot of money to acquire, and no one would want to replace his iPhone when there is a little damage to it. It is estimated that about 700 million worldwide use iPhone, and if users can buy a kit to repair small damage to their phones, I bet you they will go for it. So, you choose to include iPhone repair kits in your online dropship business, you are not likely to regret your decision.

9) Phone cases

Most people today have a phone, and the problem is that phones get damaged on a daily basis either because of careless handling or even when you exercise great care, your phone can still slip and get damaged. That is why I recommend a phone case which protects the phone when it slips and falls down.

10). Home security IP Camera

You will have rest of mind if you feel secure. With IP camera for surveillance, you can secure your home round the clock which gives you rest of mind, particularly if you are a person of great wealth. Don't forget, with the recent development in technology; you can patrol your house even when you are miles away from home because it is now possible to see the footage on your smartphone.

11). Wifi Repeater

Users of the internet are getting tired of the slow internet speed. Also they are getting tired of having restrictions on Wifi reach. Users want to use the internet without limits.

A Wifi Repeater is a solution to their problems. So, if you can promote awareness of this product, stock the quality product and charge them the right price, they will surely shop from your store and spread the good news to their friends

12). Eyeshadow Stamp

Women want to be seen beautiful at any time, and Eyeshadow Stamp makes them look pretty. However, this product has not been used widely because those that want it cannot find it to buy. Better still, those of us who would want to use it do not even know that it exists. So, what are you waiting for? Market it by promoting it extensively, and you will rake the full benefits it offers.

Other products that are trending in 2019 are the following:

- Folding mirror
- Fake eyelashes
- Teeth whitening
- Baby Diapers
- Front Facing Baby Carrier
- Men's shoes and watches
- Anti-snoring
- Customized T-shirts
- Jewelry
- Camping Gear
- Customized Mugs
- Gym and Fitness Equipment

"I believe in action, but most of all, I believe in targeted action. Only the smart ones can work less and earn more."

-Anonymous

CHAPTER SEVEN

Best Drop Shipping Companies/Suppliers

It is time to select the drop shipping companies that would supply products for your drop shipping eCommerce business. Selecting the right companies that will bring about good fortune for your business is a daunting task, so every effort must be made to minimize errors that are inherent in this kind of exercise. What you need to do is to consider the following:

- Features - What services such as pre-sale, during and post-sale services are the drop shipping suppliers going to offer. Are they going to assist you in the selection of trending products, are they going to assist in loading and transport of the products as well as accepting damaged goods.

- Product catalog - You are going to scrutinize the product catalog to see what it contains, whether the kind of products you have selected are there. Does the catalogue contain goods that are hardly available in the market or the goods that are readily available?

- Pricing - The price at which the drop shipping company sell is a factor since your profit depends on it, so choose the company the price is reasonable.

- Shipping options - What kind of shipping options are available- truck, rail, sea or air or does it depends on the circumstances of each case.

- Support services - what support services are likely to be received, such as notification of availability of new products, acceptance of damaged products and counseling when things go wrong. The list below is some of the best shipping companies.

1) Salehoo - You will have access to over 1.6 million products. They also have the biggest directory listing of over 8,000. Browsing through their platform is very easy. Just type whatever product you want to sell, Slehoowill shows all relevant suppliers.

2) AliDropship - AliExpress Dropshipping Word Press Plugin The AliExpress Dropshipping WordPress Plugin is a software that converts the WordPress installation in an online AliExpress dropship store. It helps' newbie' to become entrepreneurs instantly. You can search for the products you want to market on AliExpress.

3). Worldwide Brands - With over 9,000 whopping certified suppliers, Worldwide Brands is the safest place to work with suppliers when you are just starting a drop shipping business. The company is registered in the USA and has a lot of positive review by existing drop shippers.

4). Doba - Doba does not have huge number of suppliers, but it definitely has huge number of products – over 2 million products are being supplied on this website. Their interactive marketing system allows you to create inventory notification and provides you online support through phone calls, email services, and live chat.

5). Dropship Direct - Dropship Direct offers the best price to drop ship operators since they charge only $9.97 for their Pushlist technology; they do not charge a monthly or annual subscription fee for their services. Pushlist is a new generation data feed technology that is provided for drop shippers for automatically adding products to their catalog. With the use of Dropship Direct, your products will be packaged uniquely with customized designs.

6). Wholesale2b - Wholesale2b has the best distribution options, making it possible to place orders directly from a created website's admin dashboard. Once you partner with them to dropship their products, you qualify to place your orders directly from their website's dashboard.

7). Sunrise Wholesale - Sunrise Wholesale is seen as the best Drop Shipping

Company that can dispatch products to customers from Sunrise

Wholesale

8) National Dropshippers

This is the leading drop shippers that offers the fastest shipping speeds, in fact, goods are dispatched within one and three days. The product directory has all the categories you can choose from.

9). Investory Source - With Investory Source gives you access to its data feed, where you will make use of the feed to export products. These products will be exported to a marketplace or your website. They also have more than 1 million products, to which you will have total access.

10) Megagoods -- Megagoods is a specialty dropship company. If you deal in electronics, it is the drop shipper you need.

Its monthly fee is $14.99, one of the cheapest rate

1 1). Dropship Design

With one-time fee paid, you will be given four plan options: an eBay plan, a basic dropship plan, a data feed plan, and a website plan.

12) Oberlo - Oberlo is truly a market place for eCommerce business. Their platform for dropshipping facilitates dropshipping by linking you up with suppliers, who in turn transport products directly to consumers.

13) Wholesale Central - With wholesale Central, you can filter through categories such as clothing, electronics, and leather products.

CHAPTER EIGHT

How to Expand and Do A Profitable Business

Working for your business to expand is one of the hardest things to do to keep your business on the part of growth. However, you cannot allow your business to stagnate but to allow it to grow. There are many ways you can work to get your business to grow. They include:

i.   Add value

Don't think you are selling products to your customers, begin to think about it in terms of selling insights, information, and solutions

ii.   Work to drive more traffic to your website.

This is crucial if you want to expand since it is the traffic that turns to customers.

iii.   Be an expert.

Don't be Jack of all trade, try to specialize in a range of products, and you will be known for the areas you are an expert.

iv.   Focus on the foreseeable future

Drop shipping business is the kind of business that you should plan with long term perspective. You must commit time, resources over a long time if you want to grow.

v.   Offer extraordinary service to your customers.

Have an outstanding service for your customers. Such services like the way you settle disputes, damaged products, giving information to your customers, advice, and counseling, offering warranty and discount, and install and make sure new equipment work.

vi.   Begin today to build a solid business.

There is no short cut here about building and growing your business. Since you have a long-term view what your drop shipping business will become, begin today to invest your time, resources. That means building trust by adding customer reviews, ratings and testimonials to your website. You must also promote your business to all social media.

vii.   Invest on Facebook adverts in line with your marketing plan and to suit your budget

viii. Never lose potential customers.

They visit your online store but may not place an order on their first visit, so try re-targeting them to capture them on their second visit.

ix.   Initiate a blog aimed at driving organic traffic to your online store.

This is a low-cost marketing strategy to reach a wide target audience. It has the

potential of generating traffic and increase
the level of sales.

"Make reasonable mistakes and learn from them. Everyday is an opportunity to prove your experiences with failure. You only look and feel better about yourself."

-Anonymous

CHAPTER NINE

Mistakes to Avoid

i.   Not choosing your products for drop shipping based on research of the requirements of your potential customers.

Base your decisions on products to sell on facts and research, due diligence, making sure you fulfill the needs of the target niche. You must also monitor progress towards satisfying customers' needs; you can do this by continually encouraging reactions from the market place. Then improving customer satisfaction, which you can do by upgrading, improvements based on customers' new perceived needs and wants. So never choose your product based on what you personally like.

ii.   Selling 'fakes' that will make you rich today but land you in jail the next day.

Concentrate on selling superior products if you want to build a world class drop shipping online business.

iii.   Selling 'me too' products.

Base the products you want to sell on your conviction and what your potential customers want to buy and not because others are selling it. Evaluate and validate trends before you launch products into the market place

iv.   Setting up a generalist drop shipping store

No, you must specialize and have a target niche. Otherwise, you will not have expert knowledge to give your customers.

v.   Relying on one supplier

Never have one supplier alone because the very moment there is a problem on the part of the supplier, you cannot sell.

vi.   No patience

There is no way you can make it overnight. Don't think that way; it is a gradual process when you go into drop shipping online business.

vii.   Not handling order problems properly

It is possible that your customers may sometimes click on the wrong button, order products of the wrong quantity or size, or fail to buy. Handle such things properly and maintain a good relationship, whether this leads to a sale or not.

viii.   Not handling goods returned to you properly

If all customers buy, pay, receive the ordered item and writes a review, it seems very good. But it doesn't happen like that all the time. When your customers return goods for any valid reason, by all means, accept the items and make a refund.

"Nothing is harder than self-doubt. It may be okay to be ignorant, but knowledge without action is the world's disease."

-Freeman Kalta

CHAPTER TEN

Conclusion

Starting Drop Shipping business is easy because of its low-cost budget, but the route to greatness in the drop shipping online business is probably the most daunting task. It may not be capital intensive, but it is very labor intensive. Before considering going into the business, carry out extensive research on how it works, the cost of launching the business, potential profit, products that can be drop shipped, who are the manufacturers, wholesalers, and suppliers, and probably what pitfall to avoid.

"You are free to decide: whether you want to be among the doers or the spectators. A simple action is better than no action at all."

-DeepWord

Made in United States
North Haven, CT
24 August 2023

40691373R00045